Small Business Starters Guide

The Complete Guide for Beginners to Starting Your Small Business

I0482282

by Frank HUNTER

Table of Contents

Small Business Starters Guide

The Complete Guide for Beginners to Starting Your Small Business

Disclaimer

While all attempts have been made to verify the information provided in this book, the author does not assume any responsibility for errors, omissions, or contrary interpretations of the subject matter contained within. The information provided in this book is for educational and entertainment purposes only. The reader is responsible for his or her own actions and the author does not accept any responsibilities for any liabilities or damages, real or perceived, resulting from the use of this information.

Introduction

Running a business is not an easy task. Many people spend the whole of their life in dreaming about their own business set up. It is because there is always a difference between dreaming and implementation. Business startups require the ultimate wisdom, careful thinking, and evaluative abilities so that one can get the maximum benefit.

Businesses pass through many different phases and all these phases come up with many different ups and downs in which one needs to remain composed and serene. Among all these phases the highest amount of energy is needed during the initial phase because the proper execution of this phase can make your business flourish within no days.

The ultimate aim of any business is sure to gain profit at the utmost level but if you are starting your business then you should firstly aim at making accurate moves for the start. Profit generation comes afterward, but a right start will make your efforts fruitful. For starting a business there are multiple aspects which need to be catered and this book will help you in making these decisions.

If all these steps will be carried out in the best possible way you will surely make fame within no time. Starting a business is just like rearing a child, during child rearing you can get fatigued and distressed but once you see it growing all that fatigue gets buried under the contentment of success.

Chapter 1- Personal Evaluation before Starting the Business

Setting up a business is no less than a challenge. But entrepreneurs who have the passion and drive for setting up their own business can cater this challenge with enthusiasm and wise thinking.

No matter at which level you want to start a business, whether a small set up at your home or a big network of franchises, every business passes through the same phase of initiation and the same level of initial struggle.

Before starting up with your venture just answer the following major questions:

Idea Generation

Great business ideas are open all around you. The most appropriate way to get the best and most feasible idea for your business is to keep yourself receptive for the possibilities until you come up with one potential idea. You need to search a drop-dead idea which can set the market on fire.

Dig out your inner intuition

Running a business is not an easy task. Even if you will find some competitive idea, you will need a lot of energy and patience to take your business to the maximum heights. So while generating some idea, the best thing is to run after your intuition.

An inner intuition is the ultimate source of energy so when you will follow your instinct, the chances of gaining success are enhanced. Generate ideas from your interests and motivation so that you may not need to put up extra energy.

Look around with an evaluative lens:

Before idea generation, there is always an incubation time in which a person's thoughts and ideas keep on fluctuating and the person focuses on them one by one. Each idea is passed through evaluation and it may take several days.

But this evaluation is carried out as a mental process and no written or concrete form is established so it is better to spend this phase with a completely evaluative lens of thoughts and analysis. Look around your environment and surrounding so that you may find some feasible idea.

Keep your company creative:

Strong and creative minds always spread creativity around so being an enthusiast for entrepreneurial venture you need to keep a company which can motivate you for this venture. Try to sit in business circles and keep a relationship with entrepreneurial figures so that you may get some idea or help for generation of the idea.

You can get an idea about the current market trends and feasible ventures when you talk and discuss with these experience people.

Consider All Possibilities:

After idea generation, the next step is to evaluate this idea on the basis of practical concerns and feasibility, it is because an idea may look genuine and attractive while in the early stage but when it comes to implementation, it may appear to be the worst one. A simple process for catering all possibilities is to ask following questions and then figure out the possibilities of the idea.

What is the vision behind starting the business?

What level of business do I wish or dream of?

What is the potential customer segment as per the idea?

What specific service or product will this business provide?

How much money and time will I need to start with the business, and do I possess it?

What is the point of differentiation which makes this idea unique and feasible?

What can be the options for locating the business which can give a maximum benefit?

How much will human resource be needed for this idea to get implemented?

What kind of and how many suppliers will be needed for this idea?

How many finances will be needed to start the business?

What is the possibility of getting a loan for the business if needed?

How much initiation and gearing period will be needed for getting the business on the track?

How long will it take to reach to profit break even, is it feasible?

What is the intensity of the competition for my business?

What pricing strategy will be the best, keeping in view the current market condition?

What is the status of this idea converted into a business, from a legal standpoint?

What will be the tax structure related to this idea of business and will I be able to pay?

What is the possibility of insurance package for the business?

What kind of advertisement will I pursue this idea?

Will it be a side business or full-time activity to be pursued?

Answering these questions and writing it down will make many of the opportunities obvious to you. Merely considering an idea is not enough until you evaluate it on the grounds of possibility and feasibility will make the path clearer for the start of the business.

Assessment of External Resources

All of the resources which will be needed in the business will reside in the external domain of your business. You will need to analyze these resources for getting the best fit for your business.

Human resource

This is the biggest resource for a business, whether the business is at initial phase or is an established one. Evaluate the type of human resource which you will require. It will largely depend on upon the type of products and services selected for the business. Try to assess the labor market with highest potential and passion for joining a new venture of business

Financial resource

Obviously, these serve as the backbone for a business. Until you will reach the profit break even you will need cash flow without a break. Assess all the possible sources of resources like loans, equity, and other options

Operational resource

For starting a business various operational resources will be needed. Before entering the industry, evaluate all the needed resources so that you may not stick at some crucial phase. It is like preparing well enough earlier so that at the time of actual operation your new business venture may not suffer from any kind of deficiency and scarcity.

Legal resources

In modern day business world, this appears to be an inevitable resource which can change the fate of a business. Gather all kind of legal resources like contracts, insurance policies, license agreements and all related legal documents and services which will help your business to flourish without a pause.

Market Research

Generating the idea and looking for the possibilities is like playing into the internal environment of a business venture. But there is the external domain which really affects businesses, at the initiation phase as well as in the operational phase. Some of the important elements of market research include:

Competitive analysis

For any business, competition is the biggest challenge. Even the brightest of the business ideas can turn down into a complete turmoil if competition is not well managed. Look around the market and analyze the strengths and weaknesses of your competition. Evaluate the points at which your business can turn up better than the competition

Economic conditions

The economic analysis can be carried out at various different levels. First of all, there is a broader economy of the country which can direct many decisions related to the business sector. Then there is the economic condition of a particular business, industry and domain. Evaluate these market indicators fully.

Technology options

In this modern era, technology interplay is something really unavoidable. Analyze the market for technology options. Evaluate the ways which are in practice and think about the ways in which you can better apply these methods

Political pressures

Businesses do not operate in isolation. So if you are located in some area where there is some kind of political instability or turmoil then you need to be even more cautious about this factor. Political pressures and affiliations if any can turn the fate of your business so analyze these factors, well before time.

Chapter 2- Sample for Successful Small Business Plan

A business plan is actually a written documentation in which every aspect of the business, to be started, is mentioned with detail so that the action plan and route map for starting the business and related operations becomes clearer.

It is a kind of living document for the business which depicts 3 to 5 years ahead and mentions the details of the specific route which a company plans to follow to generate revenues.

Executive Summary

The executive summary of a business is a snapshot for the business plan as a whole and related to the profile and goals of the company.

A standard executive summary touches following major points:

- Problem
- Solution
- Market
- Competition

- Financial Highlights

Company Description

The company description delivers the information about a business that what it does, what is the point of differentiation for this business and the specific market which will be targeted by the business.

- Problem at question
- Our Solution
- Validation of Problem and Solution
- Future Plans and road maps

Market Analysis

It is one of the most crucial, critical and practical parts of a business plan which will drive your way for making your business a reality. Until a business plan is well supported by thorough market research you can never expect progress and growth.

- Market Segmentation
- Target Market Segment Strategy
- Market Needs
- Market Trends

- Market Growth

- Key Customers

- Future Markets

- Competition

- Competitors

- Our Competitive advantage

Organization & Management

While making up a business plan it very crucial to define the operations of a business with respect to the team and specific task allocated. The organization and management structure needs to be mentioned quite fully at the start of the business so that the line of operation gets clearer. Define the following items of management in the business plan:

- Organizational Structure

- Company Ownership

- Management Team

- Personnel Plan

- Company History

Service or Product Line

In this part of eth business plan, you will deal with following aspects:

- What is the item of product which the business will be selling?
- What is the point of value creation for customers?
- Describe product lifecycle

Marketing & Sales

In today's world of fierce competition and global economy, marketing serves as the backbone for a business as it can make great changes to a business. Describe the marketing plan of your business with respect to following elements:

- Market Segmentation
- Market strategy
- Market needs
- Market trends
- Market growth
- Key customers

- Future markets

- Extent of competition

- Competitors

- Our competitive advantage

Strategy and Implementation details:

In this part, you will describe the implementation details related to all those aspects which have been mentioned earlier in the business plan. It relates to the means of achieving the goals and missions

- Marketing Plan

- Sales Plan

- Location

- Facility details

- Technology

- tools and Equipment

- Milestones

- Key Metrics

Funding Request:

If you are preparing the business plan as a proposal for getting some funds from potential investors then you surely need to add this part in which you will ask the grant or fund in such a way that the investor get convinced about the practicality of the idea. The better a funding request is written, the greater are the chances to get the funds. Along with the funding request, you will also need to add the financial projections.

Financial Projections:

Although formulating the financial projections is crucial for every sort of business but it becomes even more important if you are aimed at getting some funds from an investor. The practical and feasible cash flows and financial projections will help the investor understand the business feasibility and the process of decision making will become smoother for the investor.

- Sales Forecast

- Revenue

- Expenses

- Profit /Loss(Projected)

- Projected Cash Flow (Projected)

- Balance Sheet (Projected)

- Business Ratios

Appendix:

An appendix usually appears as an essential part of any professional document as it provides a place to mention information which can be beneficial in understanding the whole document. In the case of a business plan, you can add permits, resumes, and leases.

Apart from this, the appendix is also the ideal portion of the document to attach graphs and diagrams. In any business plan appendix usually comprise of cash flow carts and bars to show progress over five years so that the pictorial demonstration can make visualization easier.

Chapter 3- Financing Strategies for Your Business

In the cooperate world as well as in the household world, the biggest challenge is to make up some efficient financing strategy which can help you to meet your ends.

Crucial factors of a financial strategy

While formulating a financial strategy for your business you need to be highly informative about following major aspects of your business idea:

- Requirements of Future liquidity requirements
- Future cash flow
- The exact level assets and liabilities
- The risk profile for the business
- Timeline for reaching the break even and implementation of strategy
- Modes of finances available
- Methods for rolling out the strategy

- Specific strategies to raise the capital

Strategies for financing the business

While formulating the specific strategy for financing your business, you need to decide the path which will be suitable for your business. You can either start it on your own or you look for means of financing your business in the outer environment.

The specific strategy for funding a business generally fall into two major categories:

1. Self-financing
2. Investor funding

Self-financing

Following can be considered as the options for finding your business on your own. You can choose any of these options based upon the suitability, feasibility and specific need of your business so that the strategy turns out to be feasible.

- **Savings**

One of the best ways to make use of your savings is to incorporate them for your passion. In the case of having a craving of business, nothing can be as good as your own savings to fund your business. Although the probability and risk analysis is equally important in the case of savings yet you need not be extra curious about paying off, if you are using your own savings.

- **Personal Debt**

For small to medium business adventures, personal debts are more feasible as compared to bank loans because these are usually without any guarantee and complicated terms and conditions. Personal debts also save the entrepreneur from the panic of approaching some bank and proving that his business idea is the best one to support

- **Family and friends**

In the case of smaller business set up your friends and family can also help you in your business. If you have a supportive circle of siblings, parents or spouse you can easily manage to find your business on your own. In this case, the trust element is high so unlike banks you need not provide any kind of security or other official documentation. Not only financial support but friends and family are also the source of emotional support for you.

- **Cash flows**

This method of self-financing can be applied in later part of the business when the business is mature enough and has started making profits. In this case, the cash flows generated by the business will be given back to the business to support important operations so that the business may not indulge in any kind of personal or commercial debt.

Investor funding

If you want to follow a thorough compliance with all kinds of financial and securities law, then you can adopt any of the fowling financing strategies for your business, this list caters almost all categories of investors available for funding the business projects.

- Special strategies for cooperatives
- Private offerings
- Direct Public Offerings or DPOs
- Fan-based funding (pre-sales, donations, memberships)

- Public-private partnerships and grants

Steps to follow in case of targeting the investors for financing your business:

In the majority of the cases an entrepreneur just has some high flying idea and when it comes to implementation, the finances become the biggest hurdles. In this case, you will need to get to some potential investor for your business idea so that your dream can come true.

Following are the basic steps which you will follow in case of utilizing a financial strategy of investor funding:

Step 1: Formulating the financial strategy

This step will involve following major steps

- **Execution plan and list of tasks**

First of all mention all the tasks in such a clear way that the whole execution plan becomes clearer for the investor to view.

Do not consider anything obvious. You will surely need to mention all the details and possibilities

- **Financial plans**

Mention the list of task in such a way that it covers the financial aspect of every task. Make every activity distinguishable enough in terms of finances so that investor can make a distinction between all

- **Financial strategy roadmap**

Mention the long term utilization of finances by the business. Set a clearer road map so that the investor finds it appealing

Step 2: Business plan with an executive summary

In this step, you will mention all those details which have been mentioned in the previous section of the book. This part basically creates a source of interest for the investor.

Step 3: Targeting and engaging the investors

- **Making a list of potential investors**

Not all investors will be suitable for your business, based on the specific idea of your business and the industry which you will be targeting, make a list of investors which can be selected as a target.

- **Formulating an elevator pitch**

After making the list of investors, formulate an elevator pitch which is a two minutes verbal depiction of your idea, so it must be catchy and concise at the same time.

Step 4: making up a presentation for the investor

This step usually comes when the investor shows some interest in your idea after listening to you and invites you to present your business idea in front of related authorities.

- **Gathering presentation essentials**

Arrange for making a presentation which is to the point and impressive. Add charts and figures to keep the listener motivated towards listening to you.

- **Delivering the presentation**

Deliver the presentation in a professional way. If you feel that you are good at numbers and planning but lack soft skills for presentation then it is better to hire someone to do this for you.

Chapter 4- Market Analysis to study competition

In modern day world competition is the biggest challenge for all sorts of businesses. Even the corporate giants spend millions of dollars each year to keep themselves ahead of the competition. If you are also starting a business, you need to perform the competitive analysis ahead of time so that competition may not turn out to be a problem for you.

Competitor Analysis:

An analysis of competitors is carried out both for strategic as well as the marketing purposes, in order to assess the potential powers and weaknesses possessed by all the current as well as the future potential competitors.

 If carried out in the real spirit, this analysis makes way for defensive and offensive strategic context to recognize the opportunities and threats available for a particular business startup.

Competitor Analysis through Competitor array:

This technique involves the following major steps:

- Defining the industry in terms of nature and the scope of the industry, both in terms of qualitative and quantitative aspects.

- Identifications of all the competitors.

- Identification of the customers for your business and defining the particular benefit which these customers expect from you.

- Identification of key success factors prevalent in the domain of the industry.

- Ranking of all the key attainment features one by one, by the weighting method, in such a way that all the weights given to the entire factors sum up to one.

- Rating of each of your competitor on the basis of each key success factor, one by one.

- Multiplication of each cell of the matrix through the appropriate weighting of factors.

Competitor Analysis through Competitor profiling:

The competitor profiling is done with a strategic rationale to make the company policy stronger. An extended knowledge of competitors provides a legitimate and powerful source of long-lasting competitive advantage.

The basic cause of competitive advantage comprises of factors like superior customer value provided in the chosen market. So when competitor profiling is applied in the competitive analysis it is actual with an aim of providing an in-depth analysis of the competitor with respect to all of the industry factors which can be crucial for delivering values to the customers.

Usually, following factors are focused in the competitor profiling:

Background

This factor deals with a number of different basic factors which are a crucial part of a company.

- **Location** of all the plants, offices, as well as the online presence if any.
- **History** of company with respect to date, key personalities, events, and major trends
- **Ownership** of the company with the organizational structure and corporate governance factors.

Financials

Depending upon a particular industry and the types of product offered by the industry you will need to focus on these financials with a customized approach. Various different financial aspects may be critical for one business but not for other so look up the competitor's financial highlights which may be useful for you to craft strategy. Some examples of financial highlights useful for competitor analysis include:

- P-E ratios

- Profitability

- Financial ratios

- Growth profile

- Dividend policy

Products

In the case of competitor analysis just knowing about the products offered by the competitors is not enough. You need an in-depth evaluation of all the products with a focus on following major factors.

- New products

- Success rate for the product

- R & D strengths

- Brands

- Strength of brand

- Portfolio

- Brand loyalty

- Brand awareness

- Licenses

- Quality control methods

- Reverse engineering

- Patents

All these factors can help you in defining your product in a better way.

Marketing

Knowing about the marketing excellence of your competitor is a way to start your venture with some safe strategy. When competitor's marketing strategy is known, you can work on a better one to attain competitive advantage in the market. Marketing details of the competitors which will be crucial for analysis include following factors:

- Ad agency

- Alliances

- Allowances

- Advertising themes

- Customer base

- Customer loyalty

- Discounts

- Distribution channels applied

- Exclusivity agreements

- Geographical coverage

- Growth rate

- Market shares

- Pricing

- Promotional budgets

- Promotional mix

- Promotional strategy

- Segments served

- Success rate of sales force

Facilities

Make a profile of all the competitors with a focus on facilities and related characteristics such as:

- Shipping logistics

- Product mix within the plant

- Plant efficiency

- Plant capacity

- Location

- Capital investment

- Capacity utilization rate

- Age of plant

Personnel:

The human resource factor appears to be one of the most competitive factors in modern day business. So focus on the personnel of the competitors, with a special attention towards the following aspects.

- Total count of employees

- Key skill set

- Management's strengths

- Style of management

- Benefits

- Employee morale

- Compensation offered

- Retention rates

- Corporate

- Marketing strategies

- Objectives

- Mission statement

- Growth plans

- Acquisitions

- Divestitures

Chapter 5- Tips to promote your small business

Business activities nowadays are more like promotional advantages in which the one with highest potential to promote the business makes the biggest progress. Today's world is a world of opportunities and you can find the opportunities only when you play a proactive game.

In the case of business promotion, small businesses need to be extra cautious because they cannot spend too much on promotional activities. Still small businesses can make a good promotional plan but using the following major tips.

- ## Use integrated channels

Relying on a single method for promoting the business can be highly risky so the best way is to use integrated channels like leaflets, classified ads, sales letters, and social media. This approach will help you to focus on all possible channels so that no segment of potential customers remains unattended.

- ## Communicate and collaborate

Every industry has a segment of specific industry players who are very active in various different industry domains, try to communicate and collaborate with such industry players. This collaboration will not only promote your business at different platforms but there are chances that you may get some greater opportunity regarding your business.

Communication and collaboration will also enhance your knowledge about industry standards

- **Social networking is the tip**

In today's world, social networking is the key, whether you are a business owner or a student. It is because the modern technology has made geographic and physical boundaries meaningless. Today you can make connections without any kind of panic and these connections can help you to achieve promotional benefit for your business.

- **Use local listing service**

Every industry has a specific listing which comprises of all the business operating within the industry. If you use this channel for promotional purposes, but can be really helpful for small businesses because it aids such a kind of business to pick up an industrial presence within a short span of time.

- **Attain the fullest advantage of online channels**

There are various different social and industrial channels for online promotions which can help you to achieve a good status for your business. These channels cost nothing but make the presence of the business highly prominent over the online world. Today if you are prominent over the web you can make miracles out of your business.

- **Multiply the referrals**

Referrals can make you rise in the industry within no time. But the real smartness lies in multiplying these referrals so that the fruit of referrals can be attained. Referrals can help you gain operational benefits and you can get across the industry with greater power.

Setting up a business is not an easy task but if you are devoted towards your passion and you have the ability to follow the professional path then you can surely attain success. Patience and devotion along with the application of knowledge can make your business excel.

Conclusion

Business and trade activities have always been one of the common activities of the human world. Even in the ancient civilizations, businesses were carried out to earn a living. So trade and business have an ancient history parallel to the history of mankind. In the case of business, just like the ancient times, even today the input and kind of efforts extended by the person running the business play a crucial rule.

It is because if anything could have been turned out good; there can be no difference between the successful and unsuccessful businesses. This is what you can see in the outer corporate world where there are business giants who have passed a whole phase of effort and hard work.

If you are also interested in starting your own business, then you surely need to plan out with a wise approach. This book is all about a business startup venture. It will provide you a discussion and information about all those aspects which can be crucial for starting a business. Just having an idea for a business is not enough.

You need to nurture this idea with the input of feasibility and practicality. Unless this is done, there are no chances for making up a successful business. Another major aspect of starting a business is the mental ability to cater stress.

If you are starting a business make sure that you are able to handle the highest level of stress. It is because businesses cannot be put into the isolated world and there will be plenty of things to affect your business. So handle all these aspects with professionalism and competence.

www.ingramcontent.com/pod-product-compliance
Lightning Source LLC
Chambersburg PA
CBHW070419190526
45169CB00003B/1331